Calmly Centered

A heart to heart journey to sooth
& empower highly sensitive souls

Suzanne Schevene Brokaw

Author Name
Suzanne Schevene Brokaw

Publisher Name
Awakening Essence

Contact Information
https://www.awakening-essence.com

Calmly Centered / Suzanne Schevene Brokaw —1st ed.
ISBN 979-8-9870219-0-3

Limits of Liability and Disclaimer of Warranty

The author and/or publisher shall not be liable for any misuse of this material. This book is strictly for informational and educational purposes. The author and/or publisher do not guarantee that anyone following these suggestions, ideas or strategies will become successful. The author and/or publisher shall have neither liability nor responsibility to anyone concerning any loss or damage caused, or alleged to be caused, directly or indirectly by the information contained in this book.

Table of Contents

Dedication

To all souls bringing more
goodness into the world
Let's wake up and
rock this place.

Introduction

As I see it, the richness of life comes from all of the experiences – the highs and lows, the twists and turns,
the vast diversity that exists here. It is in the diversity that
we are enriched. We can love more deeply, laugh more uncontrollably, and grieve more honestly.

It is called aliveness. Not a manufactured state but an authentic way of being who we are, right here, right now, in this wild and crazy world of ours. It opens our hearts, minds, and eyes a bit wider, and all things hold a bit more fascination.

And to fully embody that aliveness, there comes a time when we must turn away from the marketing industry that tells us we are not good enough, pretty enough, young enough, skinny enough, and see it for what it is. A business model that is quite successful but is hurting us personally to the degree we buy into it. We are enough. We are more than enough just as we are, right here, right now.

It is time to take a stand for the brilliant, unique, quirky Self that you are – the world needs you. We need you. I need you.

The journey of life is one of movement, of challenge and triumph, of love and expression. By expression, I mean how we navigate our lives by the choices we make based on the thoughts we birthed from the beliefs and experiences we've lived. We cannot always choose the events in our lives, but we can choose how we respond to them ... once we can see a bit more clearly and gain greater awareness.

Emotions are simply Energy-in-Motion and when we allow them to flow, they process through our bodies. But when we resist, deny, ignore, or freeze they lodge in our systems and stay there until there's an opportunity to release out.

And since stress and emotions meet in the nervous system, the impact can be devastating. Learning to manage your E-motions more effectively will profoundly affect all your systems, physically, mentally, emotionally, and energetically.

Everything has a cycle to it whether you're creating a garden, a meal, a work presentation, a daily schedule, or an annual plan. The theory of the Five Elements teaches us that harmonizing with the seasonal elements is key to staying healthy and well-balanced. Each season has its role to play in the cycles of life - a time to be (winter), a time to do (spring), a time to blossom (summer), a time to reflect (late summer), and a time to let go (autumn).

Each season also has emotional challenges and opportunities. The core emotions we often get caught in are fear, anger, pretense, worry, and grief. The layers beneath the initial emotion offer us insights but unless we can navigate the initial reactive emotion, we can't access the insights and thus get stuck in the initial emotional state reacting to life rather than responding to it.

It's not about getting rid of the uncomfortable feelings and emotions but turning towards them, with loving kindness, seeing them, being with them, and sinking in more deeply to what is there.

When we resist or get stuck in these core emotions, it isn't just our emotional aspect that suffers. Our bodymind also suffers, as does our energy and our relationships, and that suffering ripples out into the world energetically supporting more suffering.

We need balance. We need inner alignment. We need flow. As we harmonize with each season, we strengthen the gifts offered – courage, compassion, joy, gratitude, and reverence. And then, what we offer to ourselves and the world is that much sweeter.

It isn't that we must learn to love each season, but it would be worthwhile to embrace it for what it has to offer, trust the process, and appreciate what is offered. Let's learn to use the energy of the season in our everyday life.

I see superpowers relating directly to the seasons. They include Presence & Slowing Down, Curiosity & Creativity, Humor, Awareness, and Love Expressed. The more we live in and from these states the easier the gifts are to access, and the challenges lessened. We develop more grace and ease in all we do. And as we develop our internal stability and connection, we are less at the mercy of the chaos around us.

This is where our journey focuses. Enhancing our superpowers so that we can navigate from a place of calm centeredness standing in our peaceful power and gentle strength with our inner wisdom guiding us more deeply into our desired life.

How to use this journal

Make it yours. Write in it, color, doodle, and draw. There are questions to ask yourself and ideas to reflect upon. It helps your processing if you take an active role (write, color, draw, dance) while you muse over things. Let yourself be free to explore, without any agenda. Make it yours and may you create your life in a way that supports your greatest joy.

A *Life by Design*

Imagine going about your life in a way that feels nourishing and nurturing. From this place of fullness, you tend to what truly matters to you, engaged in activities that light you up, and contribute in a way that only you can.

How does that feel in your body?

The wonderful thing about this is that when you have a clearer connection within, you will find that you create for yourself a more powerful presence, greater mental and emotional clarity, more energy and enthusiasm for life and the increased ability and flexibility to hold your ground yet bend with the winds of change. And when you can respond from THAT place, shifts happen. They have to.

Welcome to the world of empowered living.

Note from Suzanne

I see you. I hear you. I am you. We have all been shaken by the world we live in, feeling it in the depths of our souls.

So how do we, amongst all this turmoil, maintain our inner peace and harmony, our joy and connection, our love and compassion? How do we live our lives in a way that supports whom we are becoming?

To say it is a journey inward is both true and challenging but if we do not find our sovereignty, we will forever be led around by the one with the most convincing story to tell.

To give up our empowerment, our unique expression of who we truly are, and pretend to be like everyone else - are you ready to do that? No, neither am I. So let's not. Let's claim our sovereignty and live as the unique brilliant souls we are and contribute in a way that only we can.

Dreaming the Dreams of Winter

A Time to Be

Slowing Down & Being Present

Winter is the season of dreams. It is a time of introspection, rest, and building inner resources. The opportunities to get stuck in fear are everywhere and it can be challenging to navigate. But when we can deepen through the fear, we have access to the courage, wisdom, and stillness, a few gifts of winter. The superpowers that help us navigate this well are Slowing Down and Being Present.

*You are who you are, but you are
never limited by that.*

I settle in, my back to the crackling fire and a creamy cup of dark roast coffee in my hands. Ah, the first rays of morning sunshine hit Mt. Adams. Stunning. I watch, mesmerized, as the light begins to dance between the mountain and the sky.

And I ponder ... what is it that I most want to express in my life? What do I most want to experience? What do I most want to create? And what do I most want to contribute? What do I most want to receive? I sip my coffee and effortlessly glide into dreaming the dreams this time affords me as I join in the dawning of a new day.

I am dreaming something into existence. It is time.

My morning coffee is one of my favorite Present Moment Pleasures. There are times when we need to find pleasure in the most basic aspects of life – sunshine, food on the table, clean water to drink – and other times our Present Moment Pleasures expand into celebrations of gatherings with loved ones or being lost in the passion of painting. They all nourish & nurture us deeply.

Embrace the pause ... and allow each Present Moment Pleasure throughout the day to soak into every cell of your being, every layer of your DNA, and every light fiber of your being. This too is food.

Notice the details whether they are the soft cozy sheets that hold you as you slumber, the early morning sips of your favorite beverage, the garlic bursts in your favorite food, the smiles of your loved ones, or a car that starts every day ....
the list is endless.

Pause to take in every single pleasurable moment and you will find them multiplying in your life. Is reading this a present moment pleasure for you? Say more on that.

In a world that seems to have a need for speed, stillness is often left behind. And yet, it is in the stillness that one opens to the depth of life, sees the true richness and diversity that exists, and experiences more of the true self.

In this moment, let go of what was and what will be. Be right here, right now. Take a slow, deep inhale and a gentle exhale. Repeat. Repeat. Repeat. Notice how you feel. Notice if anything wants to let go and relax. Notice any sensations that are calling for acknowledgment. No judgment, simply notice and be with it as it is. Know that you are held in a cushion of care. What is your relationship to slowing down and allowing for spaciousness?

What if you take time for a Peaceful Pause? Pausing is Soul Care. Take time, even 15 minutes, every day to do something that is calming and nourishing to you. Something that uplifts, feels good, and makes you smile. This will allow you to be filled from the inside so that you can contribute from a place of fullness and joy. What would a peaceful pause be for you? How does it feel to take, or even consider, a peaceful pause?

Deep presence and deep rest result in deep healing. Turning towards those fragmented parts of Self that we often want to get away from allows those parts to be held. It isn't that they need to be healed so much as they need to be held, with loving compassion, for they are doing their best to keep us safe in this world of ours. Sometimes we hear the message they must share, other times we do not. But once genuinely held and witnessed, they can energetically shift and rejoin the wholeness of our Being in forward living, no longer a prisoner of the past.

Breathe into the calm beneath the chaos – slowly, deeply, intentionally. Hold your heart. Claim "I am here, now." Allow the thoughts and sensations to arise. You are deeply loved. How do you feel about Presence? What is your relationship with Presence? Do you feel you are present with yourself and others or is your mind often elsewhere?

Can you be with yourself and all that you are feeling and sensing or are you wanting to distract yourself with something else more entertaining like food or a movie? And if so, what happens when you stay here, right now? What is feeling uncomfortable and needing to be held? Can you hold that part of you?

We live in a world of change and with change comes fear. We often ruminate over the disastrous "what if" stories completely ignoring any deeply gratifying "what if" stories.

For this week, either let them go or create your "what if" stories full of loving compassion, possibilities, and delights. What would it feel like, sound like, taste like, be like, what would you say, what would you hear others say? Feel into your delightfully juicy "what if" stories of your own design.

Slowing Down and Being Present are superpowers that are too often overlooked in our world of speed. They support good decision-making because when we're exhausted, out of balance, and confused we literally cannot make good decisions. Presence opens doors for healing and for integrating the fragmented parts of self, which are all pieces of the puzzle called YOU. They all belong.

Reduce overwhelm and constant stressful input. Considering that so much of the media is sensationalism created to evoke an emotional response in us, turn it off. Turn off the notifications, unsubscribe from email lists, close anything that beeps or buzzes, catch the news once a week on a reliable network and offset it with a good news network. If silence is too disturbing at this point, turn on gentle background music or nature sounds. What can you turn off right now that will give you a bit more quiet, a bit more space, a bit more opportunity to tap into ease?

Discern who and what gets your attention. Just because someone or something calls to you – whether it is the phone ringing or a long to-do list, you get to choose if, how, and when to respond. Consciously choose what gets in and what doesn't. What is essential? And where in your life might less be enough?

Schedule "no thing" time where there is nowhere to go and nothing that needs to be done at that moment. Take time to gaze at the dancing flames and glowing embers while the fire crackles on. Or maybe you are drawn to the sky and the possibilities that exist in all those stars, planets, and galaxies. Or get lost in a piece of art. Simply be present, allowing yourself the gift of stillness, knowing your thoughts, lists and projects will be there later when you are ready to return to them. For now, let yourself mentally mosey around. Relax. Just Be. How is that?

Winter, and the slowness that organically happens, are crucial for tending to our dreams and longings for those are the seeds that grow our lives. Dream it. Feel it with all your senses. Own it. And build up your inner resources so you'll have the energy to create it. Our cultural way of being in constant motion and productivity has cost us dearly. For a long time, it has been wearing us down, causing disharmony and dis-ease, mentally, emotionally, physically, and energetically. What can we do? We can pause, regroup, and center ourselves.

To enjoy a guided meditation relating to this section, go to www.awakening-essence.com/CalmlyCentered.

Sweet dreams ....

In the quiet stillness, my creative being awakens,
called forth by the dawn of new times,
new horizons & new pleasures.
From the wholeness
of my Being,
I respond.

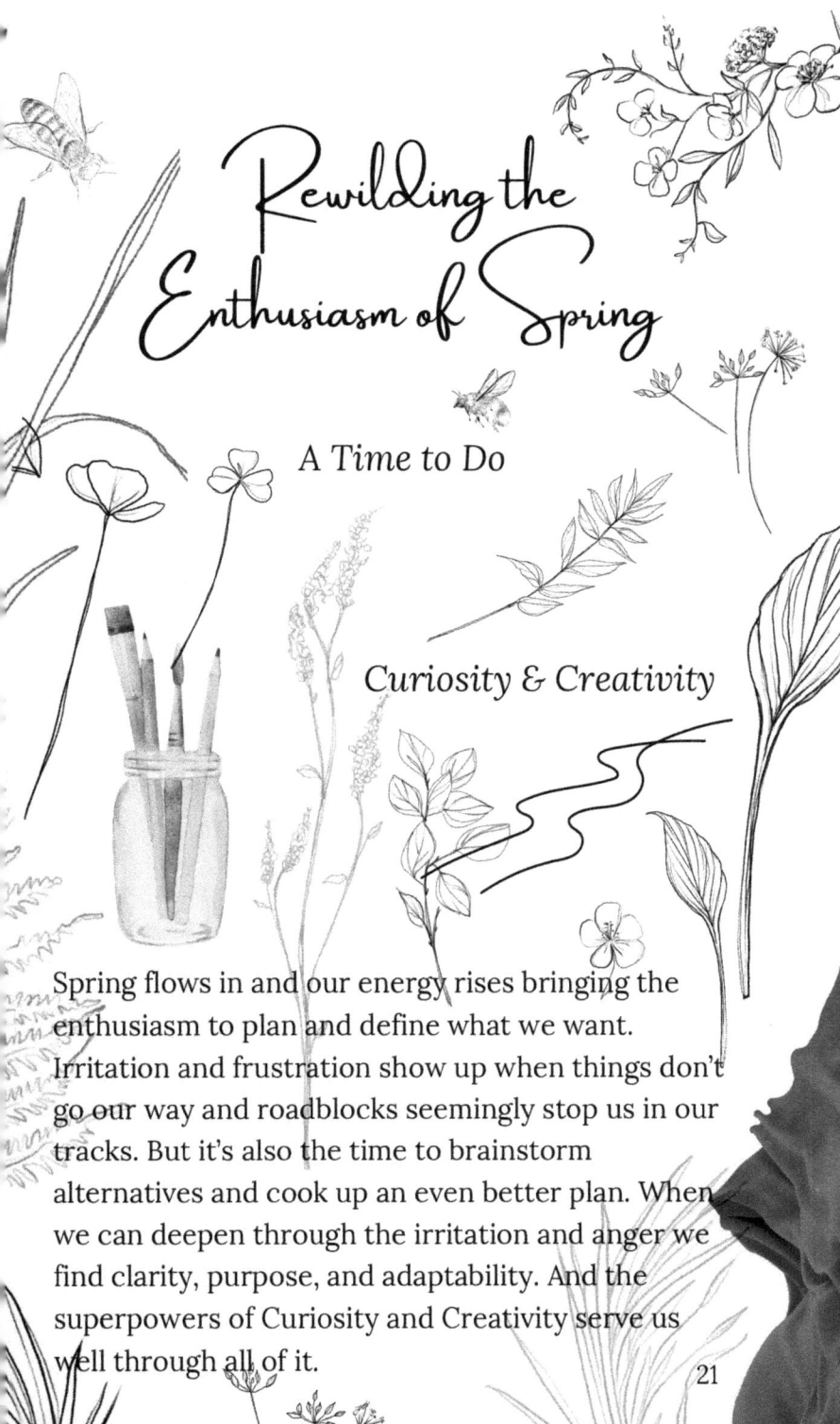

Rewilding the Enthusiasm of Spring

A Time to Do

Curiosity & Creativity

Spring flows in and our energy rises bringing the enthusiasm to plan and define what we want. Irritation and frustration show up when things don't go our way and roadblocks seemingly stop us in our tracks. But it's also the time to brainstorm alternatives and cook up an even better plan. When we can deepen through the irritation and anger we find clarity, purpose, and adaptability. And the superpowers of Curiosity and Creativity serve us well through all of it.

21

It is when one becomes curious
that life begins to brighten.

I had a concussion several months back and found it both terrifying and fascinating. I lost the ability to walk into a grocery store, scan for good-looking produce, devise a meal plan and pick up what I didn't have at home. And if I was on the computer for more than 15 minutes my head wanted to explode. There was so much I couldn't do. My. Giant. Pause.

As my healing progressed and my abilities began to come back online, I realized just how much work I historically loaded onto my mind, and not only could I not do that now, I realized the freedom in not carrying that load. I found myself choosing to do things in new ways.

What is essential and what is not? What systems can I use to plan and organize things so I don't have to keep them active in my mind? Can I limit myself to 3 projects in any given time frame (apparently no, not yet, but working on it)? I'm creating more spaciousness, more freedom, more ease, and more opportunities to live my life on my own terms as I learn to declutter and clear my mind, allowing for more insight and creative expression.

With the fresh influx of energizing spring energy, we ideally develop a clear vision from our winter dreaming and begin to formulate ideas, make decisions, determine our direction, and begin acting on our plans. But it is not uncommon to have so much going on in our minds that it gets sticky here and there.

Too much mind clutter may look like ruminating, holding on to resentments, tracking multiple to-do lists, ongoing external distractions, and constant sensory input. It uses up valuable time and energy that we could put to better use and often results in confusion and disorganization making it very difficult to see clearly, make decisions, and plan. And that, in turn, can easily
lead to irritation and frustration.

Take a moment for a check-in. Does your mind feel calm, relaxed, and curious? Or maybe revved up or stressed out? Does it feel like there is space or perhaps there's a feeling of condensed matter, brain constipation, where nothing is moving? No need to judge, simply notice. Is there a gap between how your mind feels and how you would like it to feel?

Emptying our minds regularly will help create the space needed to hear our deeper inner guidance. Of course, there is also pent-up energy in the body so walking in nature, dancing, singing, painting or something that involves whole body movement may be helpful before sitting to write. So I wholeheartedly invite you to jump, dump and rejoice!

It isn't always easy to let go. However, holding on to all that information and painful past experience is very draining, affecting health and overall wellness. It also claims energy that could be used for new projects and healthier ways of being. Do you feel as if you are overloaded? Do you want to start something new but just can't quite pull it together to start? Say more about that.

Letting it go doesn't mean we're erasing the past or forgetting what happened. It means we're letting go of the resentment and pain, and instead choosing to learn from the incident and move on with our lives. We are choosing to redirect our energy to something more desirable. Is there anything that comes to mind that you are ready to forgive and let go of? Any old grudge or resentment that isn't serving you? Any old habit, like people pleasing, that drains your energy? Where might you prefer to direct your energy?

Sometimes the air needs to be cleared with a thunderstorm. Other times, it is a more internal process to allow ourselves to let go of the emotions that no longer serve us. Try This – I'm guessing you are familiar with Tarzan and how he beats on his chest as he calls out right before swinging through the trees. Yes, I am suggesting that – well, not the swinging part. You will be positively affecting meridians, opening the lungs and if you feel around underneath your collarbone, I'm sure you will find some tender points. If it feels good to rub them, do it. If it feels good to thump on them, do it. But also, pound and give a big bellowing Tarzan call. I am not kidding. And if you have kids, have them do it too for it is a wonderful release and you'll end up laughing – bonus! Do it now. Pound on your chest and give the best Tarzan call EVER. Pretty awesome, right?

Sometimes we have so many ideas that clarity is elusive, and we spin in idea-land, never quite making a decision or choosing a path. Or perhaps we start down a path, hit an obstacle ... and then what? Quit, saying it wasn't meant to be? Push through with sheer determination fueled by irritation? Consider other ways to navigate towards our desires? It is all simply a choice in how we respond. What is your habitual way of responding to obstacles?

Decision-making can happen with more grace and ease when we are clear on how we most want to feel. How do you want to feel in your life? Sink into the experience as deeply as possible. Now think about a decision you need to make. You can use the desired feeling as a decision-making tool. Does this choice or opportunity support the desired feeling state, or does it take away from it? If it supports your desired feeling state, do it. If it doesn't, don't do it. Try it now. Or you can ask "how does it feel if I do this" and sit with it for a while. Then ask how the other option feels. Which feels better, lighter, or more right for you now? Do that.

It doesn't always make logical sense and it may take time to build a trusting relationship with yourself so start with small decisions and build from there. Try it now.

Spring requires a high burst of energy for plants to break through the soil, for us to break through the glass ceiling of our old beliefs, and for anyone to exit the birth canal. Birth takes a lot of energy! Of course there is struggle, pain, and challenge, AND a determination to live, thrive, and grow into full expression. It's the journey we all share. Our frustration, irritation, and anger show us what we are passionate about, where our boundaries are, and what we believe needs to change. Once we realize that, we can choose the best course of action and respond appropriately. Are there any areas in need of an update or a bit of a change? What are you passionate about these days? What matters to you? What is essential? And can you build your life around your answers?

Before reacting to someone or a situation, pause, take a few deep breaths, and ask 'What am I feeling? What do I need?" Listen, then respond with awareness. Feelings can only evolve if they are being felt. And then, with practice, you will begin to open the door to the deeper places within yourself that long to be heard. Ask the questions, then build the bridges.

When we are in the beginner's mind with curiosity and openness, new perspectives and ideas can flourish often leading us to even better results than we imagined. In this moment, can you simply be curious about something? No need to form an opinion, choose a side, or make a decision. Just wonder about it while you take a few deep breaths. And maybe a few more as you begin to relax just a bit more. What if things turn out far better than you imagine? What might that be like?

Being Curious and Creative are superpowers. The brain accesses the past to protect us in the future. The only time it will reach into a new future potential is through our conscious decision or some experience that puts us there or a mystical moment. Otherwise, we'll just be repeating patterns giving us what we've always gotten or shutting out parts of our lives in an attempt to remain safe. Do you have a deep inner hunger for something, even if you cannot identify it? What is your sense of it? Where do you feel it?

Embrace your curiosity and don't be afraid of what you don't know. Try seeing everything with new eyes from fresh perspectives and your curiosity will lead you to new places. You may be surprised by what you find. Are you willing to be open to possibilities beyond what you can see right now? And how does that feel?

Go outside and look around, imagining that you are seeing everything for the first time. Look at things closely as if you've never seen them before and listen to nature. Be curious and caring. Imagine you are coming across this scene for the first time in your life. What wonder might you experience?

I love the term Rewilding. What is Rewilding? It is inviting in the wilder nature of who we are. What do I mean by wilder nature? It is creative expression, pure and simple. And we ARE creative beings, so being wild refers to engaging our creativity rather than stopping it, denying it, or dimming it down. It's being more of who we are! We can be creatively wild when we write, cook, sing, garden, and problem solve or we can hold back, following the directions of others, halting our innate wildness and simply go through the motions. Rewilding, then, is choosing to embrace our creativity joyfully and intentionally. Where are you living your wildness?

To enjoy a guided meditation relating to this section, go to www.awakening-essence.com/ CalmlyCentered.

Rewild yourself, you magnificent little sunbeam!

That part of you that is anxious to get going,
to plan, to do .. the part that is having a hard time,
scoop her in, be with her. Maybe she'll tell you all about
it. Maybe she'll cry. Maybe she'll just want to be held in
silence or maybe she is hesitant to come too close and
that is ok too. It's all about beginning to build a
trusting relationship with all parts of yourself. Scoop
them in, love them and listen,
knowing they are tending to you the
best they know how.

Dancing the Harmonics of Summer

A Time to Blossom

Laugh & Be Amused

Most everyone loves summer and why not? The warmth of the sun, the bounty of flowers, garden fresh foods, and blossoming projects. The energy is high and activity is the name of the game. Joy is everywhere ... unless it isn't. Pretense is the challenge and a big one it is. But beneath that is the joy, laughter, and social events that can be so very uplifting. The superpowers of summer include Humor and Self-Amusement.

Joy is the clearest indicator of deep wellness.
It is the result of our core vitality & our
resilience. You cannot think your
way to joy. It must inhabit you.

My biggest oddity, according to my husband, is my occasional bouts of uncontrollable laughter. Let me say most of my adult life was difficult and play was a foreign word, so this is a relatively new thing for me. And what confuses him most is that it isn't always a super funny thing – it is just how my mind processes and views life.

This past summer we cruised to Alaska and eloped. While attending a presentation on Orca whales the naturalists asked for questions. The guy behind us raised his hand asking, "Do Orcas hump other mammals?" What? What? This is a family-friendly program and he's asking if they cross breed? I burst out laughing, uncontrollably, falling over in Kevin's lap. "People are starting to stare," Kevin whispered which just made me laugh harder. Finally, in control enough to confirm the question, he apparently asked if Orcas hunt other mammals, not hump them, which got us both laughing. It's the little things and the misunderstandings that get me the most. Ah life, you amuse me so.

For many, summertime feels happy and alive. And yet, for some that is not the case. They may pretend to be happy, trying on the concept of Fake it til you Make but it really doesn't work. Sure, there are times when we need to put on a smile but a steady diet of that alienates us from ourselves and others. It keeps us from real connection and real joy.

Enjoyment can be hard if one feels "not enough" and needs one more class, one more refinement, and one more planning session. What does it take to be good enough? Nothing. You ARE good enough, right here, right now, just as you are. What you offer to the world feeds them as flowers do the bees. Your smile, your act of kindness, the meals you prepare, your business – all of it is nourishment for humanity.

And it simply requires you to show up and be yourself. Be your delightfully quirky self, oddities and all, for your unique contribution to this world is desperately needed. You add to the richness of everyone around you and that ripples out into the world. Let that soak in for a moment – your *delightfully quirky self is desperately needed right now.*

Take a slow, deep breath. What do you see as your unique and delightful quirks? Consider asking your (generally optimistic) friends or family what they see as your delightful quirks. What did you learn?

Many affirmations are a reflection of what we want to manifest. And that makes sense, but our bodies know when we are being honest and when we are not. What if rather than stating the desired truth, you state the actual truth as you know it?

Since your body knows the difference and you want to develop congruency, integrity, and trust within yourself, be honest, even in the smallest of matters. Say what you mean and mean what you say. Instead of saying "My health and wellness are top notch" say "Each day I'm moving towards greater health and wellness." Or "As I deepen my self-care, my health and wellness continue to reach new heights." Make sense? What feels deliciously true for you?

How does it feel to be honest with yourself? Perhaps you notice a more relaxed bodymind? A comforting exhale? You are building self-love, self-respect and developing a relationship that will serve you very well.

Instead of saying "I don't have time" try saying "It's not a priority for me" or "My heart isn't in it" or "No thanks." We don't need to explain ourselves although if we've been saying yes for years and today we change to no, a bit of an explanation may ease their confusion – but keep it simple. We don't need to justify anything. Changing our language reminds us that time is a choice and we can choose our priorities. Choose well. How does that feel?

Clear communication can come in many forms. I went out to the garden to harvest a few things and the twin fawns and doe froze and turned towards me. They were about to jump into our Wild Child garden plot to see if anything was left (they had already eaten most of my cabbage and broccoli). I began calmly explaining to them that I didn't want them in there anymore. This went on for about a minute, then (apparently) turkey mom had had enough, rolled her eyes at the conversation, and ran directly at them, showing me all I needed to do was wave my arms/ wings and look like I was going to attack them. It was rather funny watching the turkey chase off the deer, but ... you know ... moms can get territorial and the turkey kids wanted to play in the grass. I get it. Clear Communication – a summer trait – is valuable and efficient. Can you more clearly communicate something today?

Consider levels of communication. At one level there is simply an exchange of words. "Hi, how are you." "Good, you?" "Good." The next level is an exchange of necessary information, nothing more. It's factual and to the point. "Please get coffee at the store." Many interactions stop there but if we take it one more level we get to where I want to know your perspective from you, not my idea of your perspective. I don't need to agree but I want to understand where you're coming from. How does it feel to know that I sincerely want to understand your ideas and perspectives?

And then moving into that magical place of higher-level communication, we listen for possibility. We step into the opportunity to discover something together, rather than rehashing what we already know, and thus, new ideas, perspectives, and options can arise. We both walk away feeling good, inspired, and nourished. I'd venture to say this is absolutely needed now in a time when new ways of being are required to build a better world. Flow. Ease. Discovery. How might that be?

Circling back to yourself - how well do you listen? What goes on in your inner world? Do you repeat the same thing over and over and over as though it's true without question or do you listen to your thoughts, ideas, and inspirations, being curious about new possibilities and exploring those ideas that light you up?

Often the sticky places to the realization of our dreams are internal, not external. See if this shifts anything for you.

- Make a list of the reasons you can't live your best life. (I'm too busy, I don't have the money, I'm too old, etc.).
- Notice how many of them are external reasons. For today, let go of any reasons outside of yourself as to why you are not realizing your desires.
- Close your eyes taking several slow, deep belly breaths.
- Ask: "What choices am I making that are contributing to my current experience of life?" (I say yes to things I don't want to say yes to because I want others to like me, I choose to not focus on money because I don't care that much about it, I no longer put myself out there because I don't want to risk rejection, etc.)
- What's one new choice that you could make today that will give you access to creating a different experience right away?

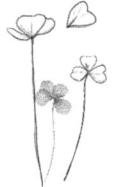

True joy arises when we are open to all of our experiences, not just pleasure. We know that diversity feeds into the richness of our experiences and if we can live from that authentic place - presence, compassion, integrity, and honesty - then joy is present. It is a state of being.

"Many of the things that undermine our joy and happiness we create ourselves ... it simply depends on the attitudes, the perspectives and the reactions we bring to situations and to our relationships with other people. When it comes to personal happiness there is a lot that we as individuals can do," wrote the Dalai Lama in The Book of Joy (pg 14). How does joy play out in your life?

Summer superpowers are Humor and Self-Amusement. I've claimed myself as a Master of Self-Amusement simply because it makes me smile and I generally find life quite funny. Some of that comes from being willing to be a beginner and compassionately laughing with myself as I stumble along. It's about holding a lighter mindset and not taking everything so seriously. Granted when I am serious and focused, I am that. But it's mandatory to balance that out with lighthearted and respectful humor.

Do you find you can be present with your current activity, whether it is focused work, laughing with a friend, lost in your creativity, or is there always an undertone of life being serious or hard or sucky?

When did we forget how to have fun, laugh, and play? I must admit it is only relatively recently that I've brought this into my life. Most of it had been about survival so if that is true for you, that's ok. It is what it is. It will simply be that much sweeter of an experience as you bring it in. What is your relationship with fun and play?

What is fun anyway? Yes, there are big fun things like vacations, day trips with the bikes, and the kids over for dinner and games but they can also be tiny simple things that make us smile. This is what I call self-amusement; solo fun that warms my heart, like my art journal, stopping when a great song comes on to sing and dance to it (definitely a solo thing), learning guitar, and writing songs using only 5 chords. Once when I was out in the garden singing, a wild peacock (peahen actually) showed up and hung out for a few weeks and yes, I sang to her most days. I consider that self-amusement because it is uplifting, makes me smile, feels really good, and isn't dependent upon someone or something else; it is self-contained. Simple pleasures every day. Soul food. Vital. How can you bring more humor, lightness, and self-amusement into your daily life?

To enjoy a guided meditation relating to this section, go to www.awakening-essence.com/CalmlyCentered.

Dance. Sing. Express yourself fully under the summer sun.

The sweet mystical flow of life
~ *alive and fresh* ~
fills every cell of my body,
every layer of my DNA,
and every light fiber of my being
as I live more of my wholeness
~ *awake and aware* ~
in my beautiful wildness (creative expression).

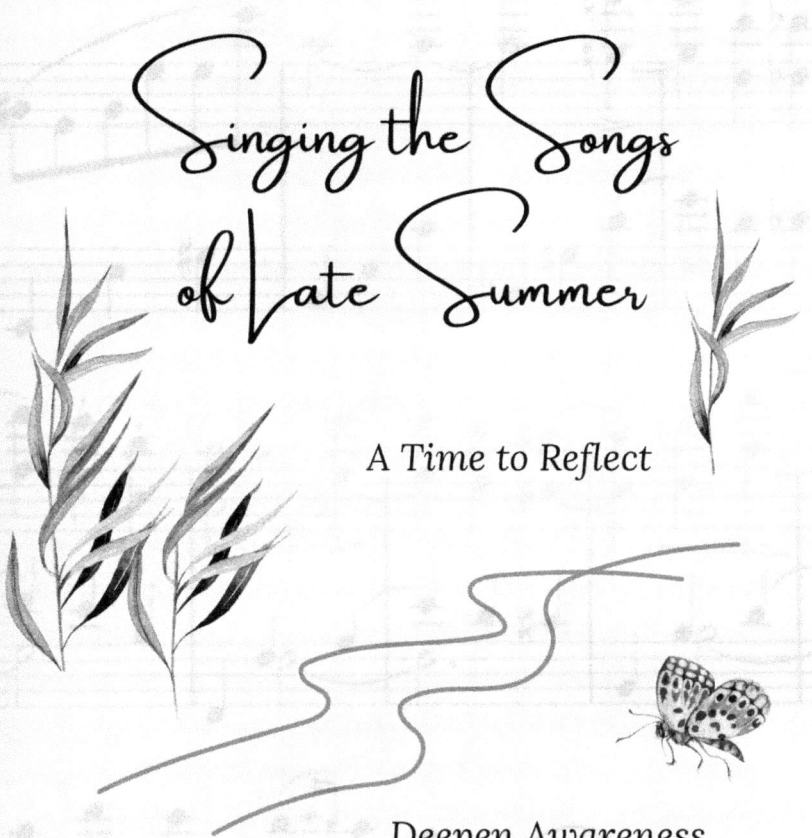

Singing the Songs of Late Summer

A Time to Reflect

Deepen Awareness

Late Summer rolls in and we have the harvest of our labors. Putting food up for the winter, counting the money made from sales, appreciation for a job well done. The big exhale ... ahhh. There's harmony within and with all of life. Now we can begin the settling-in process as we mosey back towards dreamy winter. Worry often shows up as we are concerned that the bounty will end and there won't be enough. But when we can deepen through the worry, with a stable center, our gifts are empathy, thoughtfulness, and true gratitude. The superpower here is Awareness.

Bring forth those things that touch your heart in a deep and meaningful way, bringing a sense of warmth and satisfaction to your whole being.

I feel the exhale of life ... and it never fails. As soon as the temperatures begin to drop a bit, I naturally switch to an insatiable desire to bake homemade bread and create hearty soups. I don't know if it is the alchemy of turning flour, water, salt, and yeast into a ball of living dough knowing it will soon nourish us, or the scent of baking bread that fills the house or the first slice slathered with butter that I love so much. Maybe it is the whole creative experience and the joy of knowing how much we will enjoy every single bite of it. Paired with a hearty, simmering soup, this IS autumn comfort food.

This is the perfect time to reflect on the bounty of our lives and give gratitude for all of it. But too often we go into worry – what if this happens, what if that happens, what if, what if, what if – then what? There is a plethora of reasons to worry about those we love, our health and well-being, and, of course, multiple world situations.

And yet, what does worry offer us?

We believe we're showing our care when we worry about a friend's illness but actually, we're feeding the fear of what might happen. The energy we naturally send towards them carries that worry.

From an energetic perspective, it is far more useful to imagine our friend in complete health and wellness or dancing and laughing. That will nourish them much better!

Is there someone or a situation that you would like to send light energy to right now? Imagine bright, light energy – no need to push or exert effort - simply feel the love and think of them or the situation. The energy will naturally flow where you put your attention and intention.

Worry lives in our head and centers over past or future concerns surrounding those potential stories that we don't like. We all do it at times but here's the question. Can you do something about it? If you can, go do it and let go of the worry knowing you've done your part to better the situation. If you cannot, shift your focus and energy to something more supportive. This could be getting out in nature to ground yourself in the here and now, engaging in your favorite creative activity (your brain can process in the background while you express outwardly), gathering with a group to hold space and energy for the highest outcome or talking it through with a growth-oriented friend. Realize that these supportive efforts also support a positive outcome. Utilizing your energy in positive ways will benefit you, others, and all of life. What are you feeding in your life every day? How might it feel to use your energy intentionally?

There are times we just need to live alongside it. When I finally got out of an abusive marriage the kids and I were homeless for a while. To say I was traumatized, fearful, and worried was an understatement. And it is times like this when we rise from the ashes and embrace our inner phoenix. Or we don't. The only thing I had to be grateful for were my kids. And my commitment to raising them was what stirred the fiery embers within and stood me up to take the next step. I wanted them to grow up respectful, resourceful, resilient, and responsible and to live a life of their own choosing, rather than one imposed upon them by someone else. That was my driving force to stand back up and take a step forward. Then I was able to be grateful for my kids AND the sunshine. And I built from there, one step at a time. What is your driving force, the thing that keeps you going when the going gets tough?

Whether you have a gratitude journal, make a few gratitude notes in your daytimer, or take a peaceful pause to feel the gratitude in your heart, please develop this habit. We have so very much to be grateful for in our lives and this gratitude nourishes us deeply and builds inner resources. Look for one small thing. Then look for another. You'll find it. Trust me.

Years ago, at an Arizona Native American art museum, I was captivated by a painting of two Indians sitting on a hill watching the sunset. The write-up explained this was a way of honoring life - taking the time at the end of each day to appreciate and give thanks for the gift of that day. It has lived on within me and I always find sunset a very peaceful time for reflection.

To deepen your gratitude, ask a few more questions. What really moved you today? It could be as simple as a warm smile or song that had meaning to you, the kind gesture of your partner or a stranger, or the giggle of a child. Did anything surprise you? Was something easier or harder than expected? Did you learn a new fact or gain a new perspective? Does it cause you to think a bit differently? Are you changed in some way?

When in harmony there is stability, reliability, probity and abundance. There is a giving and receiving that happens, along with healthy empathy. We're aware of our own needs and the needs of others. When we are stressed out, overgive, ignore our boundaries or act as if we have no needs of our own it costs us something – time, health, relationships, mental & emotional well-being - and we end up depleting ourselves, feeling overwhelmed, exhausted and anxious. When we develop healthy habits and tools for staying connected, our lives change. They have to.

Can we step into greater sovereignty for the benefit of all? By sovereignty, I mean being able to make our own decisions, choose who we are in a relationship with, and how much space to give them in our lives. It is having the individual power to follow our inner guidance and do what is right for us. What are your thoughts and feelings about sovereignty?

It is not easy to see someone in pain and the closer we are to them, the harder it is. Sympathy is acknowledging the suffering that is present for someone, whereas empathy is deeper due to an actual lived experience of walking in their shoes and/or the deep sensitivity to their emotional vibration. The challenge is to not take on their pain as ours and this is where education, energy management, and boundaries come into play.

Can we be present with sympathy and empathy honoring their journey without trying to fix it, change it or make it our own and instead hold a safe space, a cushion of care, allowing reflection and gratitude to surface? Can we create a safe cushion of care for others? Can we create a safe cushion of care for ourselves? What would that be like?

The superpower of late summer is Awareness. Awareness not only keeps us safe and healthy but develops our intuitive senses, our clarity, our amusement levels, and our reasons to be grateful. It helps us to know when we feel off a bit. We can then tend to our needs before they turn into something more challenging. Nip it in the bud or fertilize it with love – awareness helps with both. How would greater awareness enhance your life?

If you are aware of an unhealthy relationship you are in, be it a friend, coworker, or partner ... please get help, if needed, to make the necessary changes. Those of us who have experienced abuse didn't realize it as such at the time. When you're in it, it can be hard to see. But when something inside of you is feeling that "this" is just not right, you are probably correct. Is anything feeling "off" in your life right now? What can you do about it today?

Is there something you have always believed about yourself that life is showing you might not be true? What feels true now?

A gentle reminder that outside is all stuff that can be taken from you. Inside is where you find true safety, strength, and support. Develop your inner relationship and the resulting bounty will astound you.

To enjoy a guided meditation relating to this section, go to www.awakening-essence.com/ CalmlyCentered.

Celebrate the bounty that is you!

Stand in your peaceful power
and graceful strength and
I will stand in mine,
with you.

Listening to the Whisperings of Autumn

A Time to Let Go

Express Love

It's autumn. The apples are picked eaten, or stored for the winter. The leaves are turning, and summer is definitely over. It's that time of the year when we still long for the warmth and energy of the summer but all the longing in the world won't bring it back. We must let go and allow it to fade into the past. When we accept that and let go, we can find the sacredness in all things. Love Expressed is the superpower of autumn.

It's when we keep an old story alive that we continue to feel the pain. Otherwise, it is simply a memory.

At one point I had 3 dogs: Bear, a big ol' retriever, and 2 husky mix sisters, Sara and Dakota. Dakota clearly ran the 365-acre property in a highly efficient way, making sure the wildlife would pass on through at an appropriate distance from the house, and if they got too close, they (she recruited a couple of neighbor dogs) would go out in formation and usher them on their way. She wasn't well trained by human standards, but she was very well-mannered and strict with what went on out outside.

When I had to move to a place without acreage, I felt re-homing the girls was the best option because of their need for space. One day, several months later, I looked out my back window to see Dakota sitting in the backyard, staring at the house. She had come home, and I realized at that moment the mistake I had made in letting the girls go. She went on to teach me so much about family, love, and sharing this world with all of its inhabitants.

When she crossed over, there was a huge hole in my heart. I wasn't ready to let her go. It is with deep honor, respect, and humorous eye-rolling that she lives on, forever in my heart, as a teacher, friend, companion, and independent-thinking female. So much love.

Grief calls to us in many ways and far more often than we'd prefer. It may be a big loss like that of a loved one now gone
or a mixed one of loss & pride as our youngsters head out on their own or the smaller almost daily ones like the last of the chocolate ganache, a fun-filled evening, or the end of summer. We feel the loss.

Rather than hurrying to fill it, can we allow it to be? Can we honor what was there and hold it tenderly without needing to fill it right away? Can we trust that it will refill with love in its own time?

Pause and take a few slow, deep breaths. Can you sit with loss, be with it and let it be ok? Or do you hurry to fill the void with something or someone? No need to judge, simply notice.

Can you say to the part of you that is grieving "Hello, I am here with you now. I see you. I hear you. I am holding you on a cushion of care." Perhaps your hand is on the area that feels the pain. Be with it as it is & feel the love. Allow for your process to unfold and when you accept the loss, accept the love. To deny one is to deny the other. How does this feel in your body right now?

We don't relive the pain without effort to do so. Once pain is gone, we tend to forget it and move on (think childbirth) but when we hold onto it, we continue to relive it. Energy gets tangled and we get stuck in the pattern, which may be reoccurring thoughts or emotions that cause us problems. Energy must flow to nourish and nurture all that we are.

Expressing yourself can be extremely helpful, whether that is talking with someone, writing it out, singing ... any kind of expression helps to move energy. And those deep, unnamed feelings within especially love to have an avenue out that is beyond words such as painting, dancing, or howling at the moon. Creative expression is transformative. Honor your process. Allow for the time you need. What are your favorite forms of creative expression? Can you sense the sacredness in all of life?

Love and grief go hand-in-hand for we cannot have one without the other. Grief is lamenting the loss of what was. The love will always endure, but it has changed form. Hold it deep within your heart. Healing will happen. It is important to realize that even those things we are glad to be done with have a slight component of grief, for it is a very real part of the letting go process. It may be ever so slight. Ever so slight. Sometimes letting go is something we've wanted and is joyful but it's the letting in of new, healthy love that is the challenge. Love of Self is the place to start and build from there.

Can you feel the love that you are? Can you look in the mirror and say to yourself, "I love you so very much." Try it now and consider making it a part of your daily routine. How does that feel?

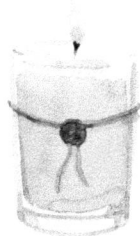

Love Expressed is the superpower of autumn. First for Self, and then for all of life. At one point I enjoyed making little paintings with inspirational messages on them. Not knowing what to do with them I decided to leave them around town anonymously. I felt a bit mischievous sneaking bits of love here and there – on windshields of cars, in the coffee shop, on the windowsill of the grocery store, the library, bulletin boards – places where anyone could pick them up. It felt good to see that they got snatched up quickly. It was a way for me to share love in a quiet, simple, and fun way. Have you ever left little uplift notes around, for yourself or others? Try it and see how it feels.

It could be a genuine smile and eye contact with the checkout clerk. Buying a bridge pass or coffee for someone 2 spots back. It could be a sincere compliment. It could be humming your way through the grocery store. When we strip away all the extraneous, we see the real value of being present with one another, expressing who we are as fellow travelers on this journey called life. Let us deepen our care, connection, creativity, and well-being as we offer bits of love wherever we are. How does that feel?

A life well lived is one we create for ourselves through our thoughts, beliefs, words, and actions. We are incredibly powerful and as we own that, we will create the world of our dreams one step at a time. It isn't always easy, but it is definitely worth it.

To enjoy a guided meditation relating to this section, go to www.awakening-essence.com/CalmlyCentered.

Live. Love. Laugh.

And so we head back into the energy of winter to restore, rest & replenish to dream the next dream into existence.

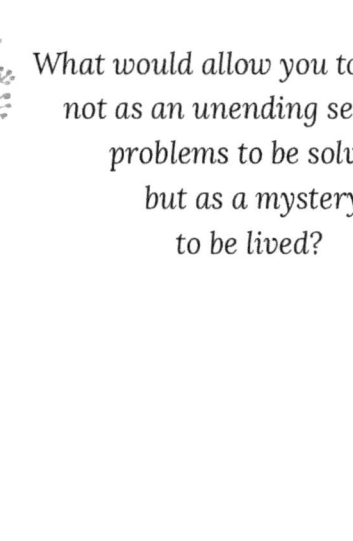

What would allow you to see life,
not as an unending series of
problems to be solved
but as a mystery
to be lived?

Conclusion

When we listen to our inner world (winter), we access peace and stillness. From there we plan with clarity & focus (spring) making good decisions and that grows good things in our lives (summer). Then we celebrate our accomplishments (late summer) and bring it all to a conclusion (autumn).

Cycles within cycles. This can be applied to possibly all aspects of life, for the one constant in life is change. Understanding the flow, the gifts and the superpowers within, may provide the bigger context to see things a bit more objectively, navigate it more effectively, and be able to take all a bit more lightly, reducing stress and increasing well-being in the process.

You may enjoy a closing meditation circling back around to our initial inquiries; what do I want to express, experience, create and contribute? Go to: www.awakening-essence.com/CalmlyCentered.

> *The most important factor in staying on our*
> *true path is to place ourselves firmly within*
> *an environment that supports the life we*
> *want to live. By seeking out people*
> *and places that inspire us and*
> *support us the road becomes*
> *smoother and more direct.*

Final Words

I hope this journey has inspired you to make some
shifts that will support a good flow of energy
aligned with the truth of who you are,
in service to what matters most.

Reflections Summary

Dreaming the Dreams of Winter - A time to Be

- Can you slow down, be present and enjoy each pleasurable moment?
- Can you pivot your fearful "what if" stories into deliciously wonderful ones?
- What can you turn off to reduce constant input?
- Schedule "no thing" time to simply Be.
- Guided Meditation Link

Rewilding the Enthusiasm of Spring - A time to Do

- Is it time to declutter your mind and let go of old stuff?
- Can you feel into your body to assist in decision making?
- What are you passionate about now?
- What is really important. Can you build your life around it?
- Guided Meditation Link

Dancing the Harmonies of Summer - A time to Blossom

- What are your unique, quirky, and delightful traits?
- Can you be honest with yourself & others, in even the smallest of matters?

- Can you communicate clearly and accurately?
- Is play and fun a part of your life?
- Guided Meditation Link

Singing the Songs of Late Summer - A time to reflect

- What are you feeding in your life every day?
- What is your driving force when things get hard?
- Can you create a safe cushion of care for yourself and others?
- Is there something you've believed about yourself that you know now is not true?
- Guided Meditation Link

Listening to the Whisperings of Autumn - A time to Let Go

- Can you be with a loss without needing to fill in the void?
- Can you honor what was, feeling both the loss and the love?
- Can you look in the mirror and express your love?
- Can you express love to a fellow traveler in the journey of life?
- Guided Meditation Link

Acknowledgment

It takes a village. How can I possibly list and thank
everyone who has impacted me, all contributing
to who I am in this moment?

Know that I am in deep appreciation for all of you
with whom I've had the pleasure of interacting
with, learning from or with, teaching to or
with, or bumping into along the journey.
You are a gift to me. Thank you
from the depth of my soul.

About Suzanne

Suzanne Schevene Brokaw has been in the health and wellness field since the early 90s as a Practitioner and Instructor. Her passion is helping others foster greater awareness, empowerment, and optimal well-being in the wholeness of who they are.

She is known for her gentle presence and quiet approach to joyful living. When she isn't working on a beloved project you will find her exploring the power of intentional creativity through writing, painting, music, or cooking, enjoying the surrounding nature, inching towards slow living, or laughing at some silliness.

To see what she is serving up, visit www.awakening-essence.com.

www.ingramcontent.com/pod-product-compliance
Lightning Source LLC
Chambersburg PA
CBHW051641120626
46551CB00014B/2173